This book belongs to

_____

Published September, 2015

I LOST SOMEONE SPECIAL

ISBN: 978-1-944143-00-8

Author: Mrs. Bracha Goetz
Illustrator: Mrs. Chani Judowitz
Design and Layout: Mrs. Raizy Flamm

This book is based on the story
Let's Do A Mitzvah for Bubby and Zaidy
by Mrs. Robin Davina Meyerson

Distributed by
The Judaica Press, Inc
123 Ditmas Avenue, Brooklyn, NY 11218
718.972.6200 / 800.972.6201
info@JudaicaPress.com / JudaicaPress.com

I Lost Someone Special

Mitzvos We Can Do in Memory of a Loved One

WRITTEN BY:
BRACHA GOETZ

ILLUSTRATED BY:
CHANI JUDOWITZ

Dear Parents עמו"ש,

As a natural part of life, the transition from this world to the next is a topic to which children will at some point be introduced, whether through personal loss, national loss or even as part of a *parshah* or history lesson. With proper education, we can help our children see the journey to the next world for what it is – a transition for the *neshamah*, and at the same time, a transition for our relationship with that *neshamah*. We may be sad, but we're not cut off, since there is so much we can do to benefit the deceased.

Allow this book to open a dialogue between you and your child about ideas he or she can implement as a *zechus* for a loved one – a beloved grandparent or anyone who has passed on to whom he or she feels a connection – and about topics that are basic to our *emunah*: *Olam Haba*, the purpose of our sojourn in this world and what we can do for the deceased from our place here in *Olam Hazeh*. For while your child might be young, there are many ways in which he or she *can* make a difference to the *neshamah* of the deceased: studying *Mishnah*, performing acts of *chessed,* setting up a *gemach* for friends or classmates; these kinds of projects can be done by children of all ages.

I would like to thank those people whose efforts made this book possible: **Mrs. Bracha Goetz**, who handled a difficult topic with her trademark creativity and sensitivity; **Mrs. Chani Judowitz**, whose colorful, appealing illustrations brought these concepts to life; **Mrs. Robin Meyerson**, whose original work was the inspiration for this publication; **Mrs. Raizy Flamm**, for the beautiful layout; **Mrs. Rivkah Schachnow**, for her editorial input; **Rabbi Dr. Dovid Fox** and the Project Chai team for their invaluable feedback; and **Rav Noach Orlowek** for his careful attention to every detail of the text and illustrations and insightful recommendations toward ensuring the ultimate effectiveness of this book. A heartfelt thank you to **Mr. Mark Scherer** for generously dedicating this volume.

13 Ellul, 5775

א. ה"יק ע"ס

Rabbi Moshe Haikins
Founder and President
Chevrah Lomdei Mishnah/The Society for Mishnah Study

I lost someone special.

It's very hard for me.

He won't be coming to visit us.

How different things will be.

Mommy explained that he got some rewards here,

But now he can get all the rest.

And a *neshamah* returns to *Hashem*

At the time that is the best.

His *neshamah* lasts forever,

Even though it can't be seen,

And my *neshamah* stays
connected with his.

I'll show you
what I mean.

When *neshamos* go back to

The source of love, *Hashem*,

They ask *Hashem* to help us.

Blessings can come
because of them.

Our special connection continues.

We can give to *them*, too,

In so many caring ways –

It's amazing how much we can do!

For instance,
I can think about

Mitzvos he did a lot.

Then I can do them, too.

Here's an idea I just got!

He told me *parshah* stories,

And his smile brightened my days.

Now I tell *parshah* stories,

And try to keep his cheerful ways.

I also give *tzedakah*.

Before *Shabbos*
is a great time,

So his *neshamah* can
have an *aliyah*!

That means
I help him climb —

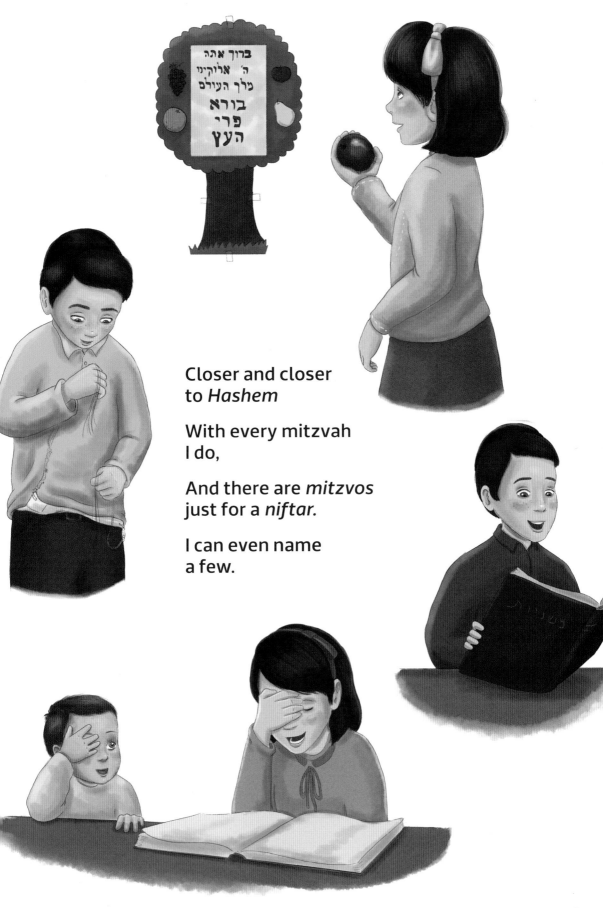

Closer and closer
to *Hashem*

With every mitzvah
I do,

And there are *mitzvos*
just for a *niftar*.

I can even name
a few.

9

People sit *shivah*

And say *Kaddish* for those who have passed

From this world into the next,

Where *mitzvos* always last.

הַמָּקוֹם יְנַחֵם אֶתְכֶם
בְּתוֹךְ שְׁאָר אֲבֵלֵי
צִיּוֹן וִירוּשָׁלָיִם:

Some visit the *kever*
on a *yahrtzeit*

And place a stone
on top.

The rock shows
we remember still.

Our caring
does not stop.

I can learn a *Mishnah*,

Which helps each *neshamah* so.

Every letter of Torah I learn

Helps our connection grow.

He is now in *Olam HaEmes*,

In a world that's pure and true,

And I feel our bond gets stronger

With each mitzvah that I do.

Someday a baby may be born

Who will receive his name.

He may not look just like him,

And his voice may not sound the same.

But hopefully he'll be able

To honor the name so fine.

Then both of their *neshamos*

Will more brightly shine!

I know that there will still be times
When I will want to cry.
Mommy said that is normal.
It's sad to say good-bye.

I can no longer stand up for him

Or give him a goodnight kiss.

But there still are lots of ways

I can care for the one I miss.

Since he can no longer do *mitzvos*

With his hands or mouth or feet,

I can follow in his footsteps,

Continuing on his path so sweet.

And each time I do a mitzvah

With him in my mind,

The special someone that I lost,

In my heart I will find.

19

And now you know
what you can do

When you can no longer
hug or touch,

Because you have just
read this book

About someone
you love so much.

Glossary

Aliyah – Going upward

Hashem – The Name: a designation for, but not the actual name of G-d

Kaddish – The prayer said by mourners in praise of G-d

Kever – A grave

Mishnah – The Oral Torah

Mitzvos – Instructions for living that G-d gave to us

Neshamah (pl. neshamos) – Soul(s)

Niftar – Someone who passed away

Olam HaEmes – The World of Truth; the next world

Parshah – The portion of the week from the Five Books of Moses

Shabbos – Our holy Sabbath, Friday night and Saturday

Shivah – A week-long mourning period

Torah – Wisdom from G-d that Jewish people study

Tzedakah – Giving a just amount of money to a worthy cause

Yahrtzeit – The Hebrew anniversary date of someone who passed away

You can learn a *Mishnah* right now, in memory of a loved one.

*If learning on behalf of a **man** who was* niftar:	*If learning on behalf of a **woman** who was* niftar:

הֲרֵינִי לוֹמֵד מִשְׁנָה זוֹ לְקַיֵּם מִצְוַת עֲשֵׂה שֶׁל תַּלְמוּד תּוֹרָה. וִיהִי רָצוֹן שֶׁיִּהְיֶה לִזְכוּת נִשְׁמַת

(Hebrew first name of the *niftar*)

בֶּן

(Hebrew first name of the *niftar*'s father)

I am learning this *Mishnah* to fulfill the mitzvah of studying Torah. Please, *Hashem*, may this bring merit for the soul of

(Hebrew first name of the *niftar*)

son of

(Hebrew first name of the *niftar*'s father)

הֲרֵינִי לוֹמֵד מִשְׁנָה זוֹ לְקַיֵּם מִצְוַת עֲשֵׂה שֶׁל תַּלְמוּד תּוֹרָה. וִיהִי רָצוֹן שֶׁיִּהְיֶה לִזְכוּת נִשְׁמַת

(Hebrew first name of the *nifteres*)

בַּת

(Hebrew first name of the *nifteres*'s father)

I am learning this *Mishnah* to fulfill the mitzvah of studying Torah. Please, *Hashem*, may this bring merit for the soul of

(Hebrew first name of the *nifteres*)

daughter of

(Hebrew first name of the *nifteres*'s father)

This *Mishnah* is the 16th (in some places it is the 21st) *Mishnah* in the 4th chapter of *Pirkei Avos*, Ethics of the Fathers.

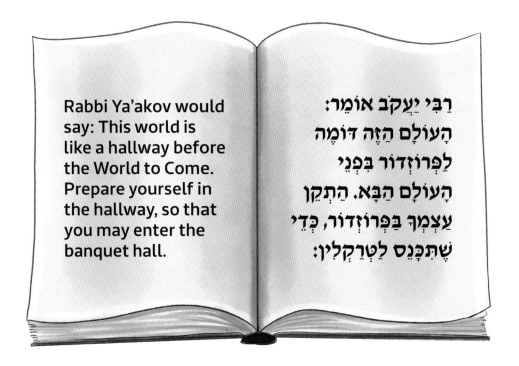

Rabbi Ya'akov would say: This world is like a hallway before the World to Come. Prepare yourself in the hallway, so that you may enter the banquet hall.

רַבִּי יַעֲקֹב אוֹמֵר: הָעוֹלָם הַזֶּה דּוֹמֶה לִפְרוֹזְדוֹר בִּפְנֵי הָעוֹלָם הַבָּא. הַתְקֵן עַצְמְךָ בַּפְּרוֹזְדוֹר, כְּדֵי שֶׁתִּכָּנֵס לַטְּרַקְלִין:

```
┌─────────────┐
│             │
│    PASTE     │
│   PICTURE    │
│    HERE      │
│             │
└─────────────┘
```

_____

_____

_____

_____

If you would like, you can put a picture of your loved one in the frame above.

Then you can write his or her name on the line beneath it.

Is there a mitzvah you would like to do to help his or her neshamah have an aliyah?

You can choose more than one mitzvah to do. Writing them down on this page can help you remember what you chose.

If there is more than one special person you would like to remember in this way, you can simply copy this page to use as many times as you would like.

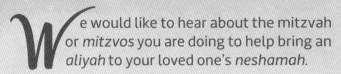

We would like to hear about the mitzvah or *mitzvos* you are doing to help bring an *aliyah* to your loved one's *neshamah*.

Here's what you can do:

Using the form below, send us the name of your loved one and write down how you are related to this special person.

Describe the mitzvah you are doing. If it is a learning program, you can tell us what it is that you are learning.

Don't forget to include your name and address so we can send you a personalized **CERTIFICATE** and colorful **STICKERS**. As part of our **MISHNAH MESSAGES** program, you will also receive interesting incentives throughout the year.

We look forward to hearing from you.

Make a copy of this page, fill in your information, and send it to us:
MAIL: Chevrah Lomdei Mishnah, 40 East 13th Street, Lakewood NJ 08701
FAX: 732.520.6483 | EMAIL: info@ChevrahLomdeiMishnah.org

AS A *ZECHUS* (MERIT) FOR THE *NESHAMAH* OF:

_____

Fill in the name of the niftar *and how you are related (if the* niftar *is a relative).*

_____

_____

Briefly describe the learning program or mitzvah you are doing.

NAME:_____

ADDRESS: _____

CITY/STATE/ZIP: _____

PHONE:_____ AGE: _____